Drum Primer
Book for Beginners

by
Tim Wimer

For Video & Audio Access, go to this address on the internet:

cvls.com/extras/drum/

HOW TO USE THIS COURSE

To use the book along with the Online Video, follow these suggestions.

Step 1

Watch a section of the Video. Rewind and watch again until you understand the material completely. (A section would be from one title page to the next).

Step 2

Once you understand the section, go to the book to practice the exercises and songs over and over until you are comfortable with them.

Step 3

After practicing with the book, go back to the Video and play along to make sure you are performing the material properly.

This course is designed to be worked through, stopping and practicing each section until you are thoroughly familiar with it. It will probably take the average beginning student 2 - 4 months to work all the way through the book and Video, so don't get in a hurry. Take your time and learn the material correctly.

DEDICATION

This book is dedicated to my wife, Funda for her support during this project.

INTRODUCTION

The *Drum Primer Book for Beginners* with Video & Audio Access is an instructional Kindle book designed for the beginning student who desires a clear, step-by-step method of learning to play the drums. Many photographs are included to make this clear and easy to understand. All music is written in standard music notation, resulting in the student being able to use other instructional material upon completion of this course. The book contains familiar songs and many techniques and exercises to help establish a firm foundation and background so necessary in learning to play any instrument.

The Video that accompanies this book will enable the student to learn 3 or 4 times faster than with other methods. This Video provides the accent, tone, and rhythm for all the songs and exercises in this book and you will progress even faster because you will be able to see the correct movements of the left and right hand.

THE AUTHOR

Tim Wimer began drumming during the late 1970's in his school band program. Since then, he has played in rock, pop, country, jazz, blues, and orchestral bands, including the 82nd Airborne Division Band, where he served as a paratrooper and musician. He currently lives in Roanoke, Virginia, where he teaches privately and works with school band programs. He has written two other books, *Drum Styles* and *Ten Lessons In Rudiments & Rhythms*, and has recorded the *Snare Drum Rudiments DVD*.

WATCH & LEARN PRODUCTS REALLY WORK

25 years ago, Watch & Learn revolutionized music instructional courses by developing well thought out, step-by-step instructional methods combined with clear, easy-to-understand graphics that were tested for effectiveness on beginners before publication. This concept, which has dramatically improved the understanding and success of beginning students, has evolved into the Watch & Learn mastermind of authors, editors, teachers, and artists that continue to set the standard of music instruction today. This has resulted in sales of almost 1.5 million products since 1979. This high quality course will significantly increase your success and enjoyment while playing the drums.

VIDEO & AUDIO ACCESS

For Video & Audio Access to all the media in this course, go to this address on the internet:

cvls.com/extras/drum/

TABLE OF CONTENTS

APPENDIX

SECTION 1
GETTING STARTED

For Video & Audio Access, go to this address on the internet:

cvls.com/extras/drum/

PARTS OF THE SNARE DRUM

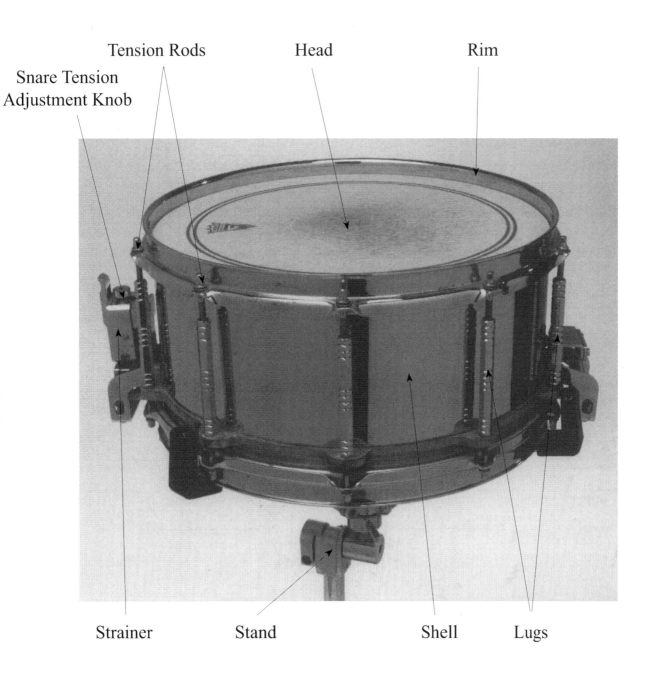

Tension Rods   Head   Rim

Snare Tension
Adjustment Knob

Strainer   Stand   Shell   Lugs

Make sure the drum heads are not torn or damaged, and that the lugs and tension rods are intact and properly tightened. Also, the drum stand should be in good working order.

1

PARTS OF THE DRUM SET

Crash Cymbal Hi Tom Medium Tom Ride Cymbal

Hi Hat Cymbals Snare Drum Bass Drum Floor Tom Cymbal Stand

Hi Hat Stand Bass Pedal

The number of drums and cymbals may vary from set to set. A standard set consists of a snare drum, bass drum, hi tom, medium tom, floor tom, hi hat cymbals, ride cymbal, and crash cymbal. You will also want to purchase a stool to sit on while playing.

CHOOSING DRUMSTICKS

You should choose drumsticks which fit your hands. If you have small hands, purchase thinner sticks such as 5A or 7A. If you have large hands, you will find that thicker sticks, such as 5B or 2B feel more comfortable. Drum sticks are generally the same length, but some are heavier than others. Choosing a weight is largely preference.

If you plan to play the drum set, you may wish to purchase sticks that have a nylon tip, which allows for a clearer sound on the cymbals.

HOLDING THE STICKS

The sticks can be held several ways, traditional grip or matched grip. Since it is easier to master, we recommend that beginners learn to hold the sticks matched grip, as explained below.

1st: Lay the stick across the palm of your hand about two inches from the butt end.

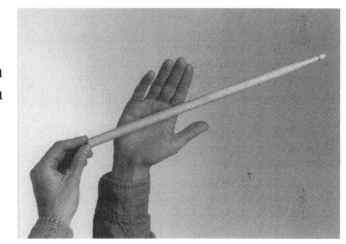

2nd: Curl your fingers around the stick. Don't grasp the stick tightly, but rather allow your fingers to gently support the stick. The thumb should be placed on the side of the stick, about even with the first finger.

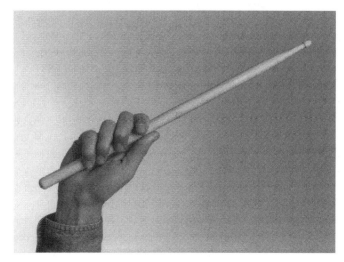

3

3rd: Rotate your wrist so that the top of your hand is toward the ceiling.

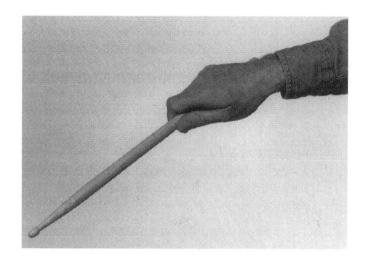

Together, the sticks should form an arrow which points in front of you. Once again, the top of the hands should be toward the ceiling.

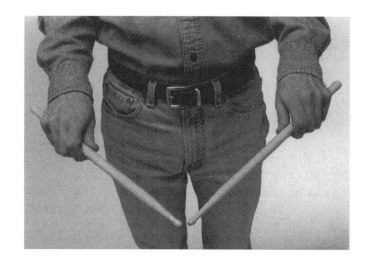

As you play, you should use your wrist, not your arms, to move the stick toward the drum. Look at the Video for the correct hand movement.

BODY POSITION

When playing in an orchestra or marching band, drummers use a standing position. While playing a drum set, drummers use a sitting position. Either way, the proper body position is similar.

The drum should be at about waist level so that you don't have to bend or reach to strike the drum. Your elbows should rest comfortably at your sides.

Standing Position

Sitting Position

5

GETTING A GOOD SOUND

To get a good sound, strike the drum in the center of the head. If one stick strikes near the center of the head and the other strikes near the edge of the head, you will hear two different tones. It may be helpful to draw a quarter-sized circle in the center of the head as a target zone.

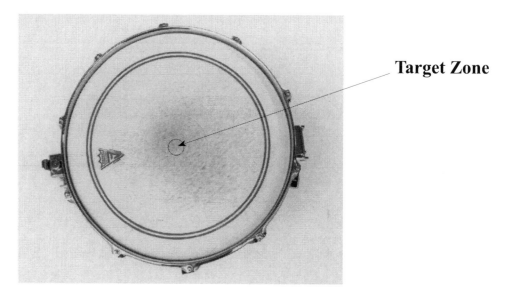

Target Zone

To prevent the tom-toms from over-ringing and sounding hollow, you may wish to purchase muffling devices, such as Dead Ringers or Zero Rings. They are inexpensive and fairly easy to install. You can get them at your local music store.

You will want to muffle your bass drum so that it produces a deep thud-like sound. Remove the tension rods, rim and head, then place a pillow or blanket inside. Make sure the pillow or blanket rests against the heads, which will prevent ringing.

Pillow or blanket

SECTION II
STICK CONTROL

For Video & Audio Access, go to this address on the internet:

cvls.com/extras/drum/

RUDIMENTS

As a beginning drummer, you are sure to discover several things: first, that your hands won't always do what you want them to do, and second, that you have a weaker hand which is more difficult to control. Right handed players can expect to have more trouble with the left hand, and left handed players can expect to have more trouble with the right hand.

By practicing sticking exercises known as rudiments, drummers can teach their hands to do what their brain wants them to do. Practicing rudiments is the key to gaining hand-to-hand coordination and speed.

When practicing the following rudimental exercises, remember these tips:

* Rudiments should be practiced on a snare drum or drum pad.

* Practice rudiments for at least 15 minutes every day. They work well as warm-ups, so spend the first part of each practice session playing them.

* Repetition is the key to achieving stick control. Try to play each rudiment or exercise for at least one minute before stopping.

* As you become more comfortable with the exercises, try to play them faster. Get a little bit faster each day.

The R stands for right stick, and the L stands for left stick.

R = Right stick   L = Left stick

The R's and L's are placed on a music staff showing quarter notes. For now, play everything at a smooth, even speed. For a more complete explanation of music notation, see Section III.

Note: There are several extra exercises in the book that are not included in the Video because of time constraints. Make sure you practice all of these extra exercises along with the Audio Tracks.

For Video & Audio Access, go to this address on the internet:

http://cvls.com/extras/drum/

Note: Play the rudiments and exercises along with the Video or Audio Tracks to make sure that your rhythm is correct.

RUDIMENT #1 - THE SINGLE STROKE ROLL

RUDIMENT #2 - THE DOUBLE STROKE ROLL

EXERCISE 1

Single & Double stroke combination (leading with the right).

EXERCISE 2

Single and Double stroke combination (leading with the left).

RUDIMENT #3 - THE SINGLE PARADIDDLE

The Single Paradiddle incorporates an accent mark (>). Accented notes are to be played louder than unaccented notes.

9

Play the following exercises along with the Video or Audio Tracks.

EXERCISE 3

Single Paradiddle and Single Stroke Roll combination (leading with the right).

R L R R   L R L L   R L R L   R L R L

EXERCISE 4

Single Paradiddle and Single Stroke Roll combination (leading with the left).

L R L L   R L R R   L R L R   L R L R

EXERCISE 5

Single Paradiddle and Double Stroke Roll combination (leading with the right).

R L R R   L R L L   R R L L   R R L L

EXERCISE 6

Single Paradiddle and Double Stroke Roll combination (leading with the left).

L R L L   R L R R   L L R R   L L R R

EXERCISE 7

Single Paradiddle, Single Stroke Roll, Double Stroke Roll combination (leading with the right).

R L R R   L R L L   R L R L   R R L L

EXERCISE 8

Single Paradiddle, Single Stroke Roll, Double Stroke Roll combination (leading with the left).

L R L L   R L R R   L R L R   L L R R

RUDIMENT #4 - THE DOUBLE PARADIDDLE

The Double Paradiddle is created by adding two notes onto the Single Paradiddle. Like the Single Paradiddle, the Double Paradiddle has an accent mark on each beginning note.

R L R L R R   L R L R L L

RUDIMENT #5 - THE TRIPLE PARADIDDLE

The Triple Paradiddle is created by adding notes onto the Double Paradiddle. Like the Single and Double Paradiddle, the Triple Paradiddle has an accent mark on each beginning note.

R L R L R L R R   L R L R L R L L

EXERCISE 9

Triple Paradiddle and Double Stroke Roll combination.

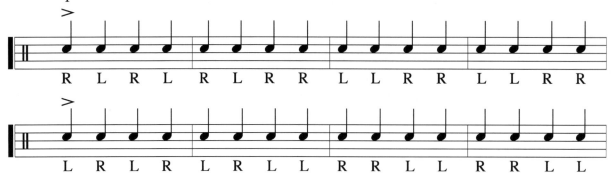

EXERCISE 10

Single and Triple Paradiddle combination.

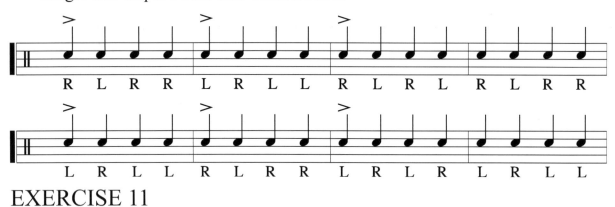

EXERCISE 11

Eight measure combination. Make sure you play along with the Audio Tracks.

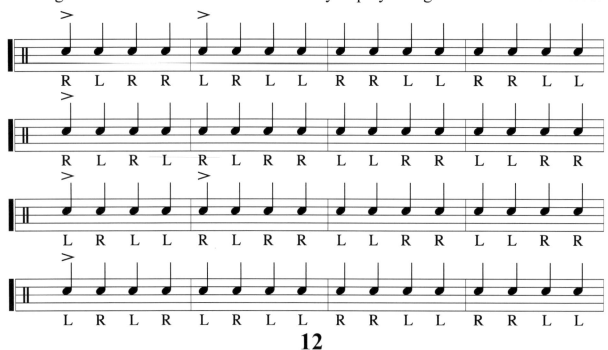

SECTION III
RHYTHMS

For Video & Audio Access, go to this address on the internet:

cvls.com/extras/drum/

Since a drummer is primarily a rhythm maker, you must understand how rhythms are created, counted, and played. In Section III, you will learn whole, half, quarter, eighth, and sixteenth notes, as well as many rhythmic combinations that can be created from these notes.

TERMS AND SIGNS

Before learning about notes, you must become familiar with a few musical terms and concepts.

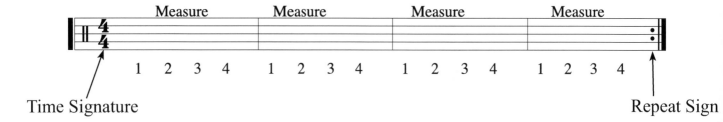

A MEASURE is a subdivision within a line. Four measures are shown above.

A TIME SIGNATURE is a fractional number which tells you how many beats can fit into each measure. In 4/4 time, 4 beats (no more and no less) will be put into each measure. The beats will be counted 1 2 3 4. Music can be written in other time signatures, but 4/4 is the most common. All the exercises in this book use 4/4 time.

A REPEAT SIGN indicates that you should repeat a previous passage. After you play the final measure, you should return to the beginning and replay the entire exercise. Remember, repetition is important when learning to play any instrument.

After playing all of the exercises in the following section along with the Video or Audio Tracks, you should have a clear understanding of musical notation.

WHOLE NOTES

The first type of note you will learn is called the whole note. Because it looks like an egg, the whole note is easy to recognize. Each whole note takes up 4 beats, so only one of them will fit into each measure.

While playing whole notes, you will strike the drum on beat 1, while beats 2, 3, and 4 will only be counted.

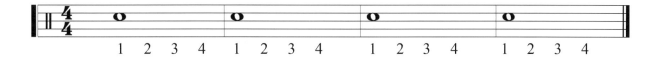

HALF NOTES

The half note looks much like the whole note, except the half note has a stem attached to its side. Each half note takes up 2 beats, so two of them will fit into each measure.

While playing half notes, you will strike the drum on beats 1 and 3, while beats 2 and 4 will only be counted.

EXERCISE 12

This exercise combines whole and half notes.

15

QUARTER NOTES

Quarter notes look much like half notes, but quarter notes are solid, rather than hollow. Each quarter note takes up 1 beat, so four of them will fit into each measure.

When playing quarter notes, you will strike the drum on beats 1, 2, 3, and 4.

EXERCISE 13

We'll combine quarter and whole notes in this exercise.

EXERCISE 14

Now we'll use quarter and half notes.

EXERCISE 15

This exercise uses quarter, half, and whole notes.

EXERCISE 16

Here we'll use quarter and half notes within the same measure.

EXERCISE 17

Here's another possible combination.

EIGHTH NOTES

Eighth notes look much like quarter notes, except eighth notes are grouped together by a single line at the top of their stems. Individual eighth notes are written with a single flag attached to the stem.

Eighth notes get 1/2 of a beat each, so 8 of them will fit into each measure. Eighth notes are counted 1 & 2 & 3 & 4 & and are played twice as fast as quarter notes.

EXERCISE 18

This exercise combines quarter and eighth notes.

17

EXERCISE 19

Here are quarter and eighth notes within the same measure.

EXERCISE 20

Now an exercise combining whole, half, quarter, and eighth notes.

SIXTEENTH NOTES

Sixteenth notes look much like eighth notes, except sixteenth notes are grouped together by a double line at the top of their stems. When written individually, a sixteenth note has a double flag attached to its stem.

Sixteenth notes get 1/4 of a beat each, so 16 of them can fit into each measure. They are counted 1 e & a 2 e & a 3 e & a 4 e & a, and are played twice as fast as eighth notes.

EXERCISE 21

This exercise combines eighth and sixteenth notes.

EXERCISE 22 (RHYTHM ONE)

Here we'll use eighth and sixteenth notes within the same measure.

1 & 2 & 3 e & a 4 e & a

EXERCISE 23

Now combine quarter, eighth, and sixteenth notes.

1 2 3 4   1 & 2 & 3 & 4 &   1 e&a 2 e&a 3 e&a 4 e&a

EXERCISE 24

Next, quarter, eighth, and sixteenth notes within the same measure.

1 & 2 & 3 e & a 4

EXERCISE 25 (RHYTHM TWO)

Another possible rhythmic combination.

1 & 2 3 e & a 4

EXERCISE 26 (RHYTHM THREE)

Yet another possibility.

1 e & a 2 & 3 e & a 4

EXERCISE 27 (RHYTHM FOUR)

Now we are going to combine Exercises 24 and 25 to create a two measure rhythm.

1 & 2 & 3 e & a 4 e & a   1 & 2   3 e & a   4

EXERCISE 28 (RHYTHM FIVE)

This time we will combine Exercises 25 and 26 to create a two measure rhythm.

1 & 2   3 e & a   4   1 e & a 2 & 3 e & a 4

After you become comfortable with the rhythms presented here, get creative and invent your own. Write them down on paper, think about how they are counted, then play them.

For Video & Audio Access, go to this address on the internet:

cvls.com/extras/drum/

SECTION IV

PLAYING THE DRUM SET

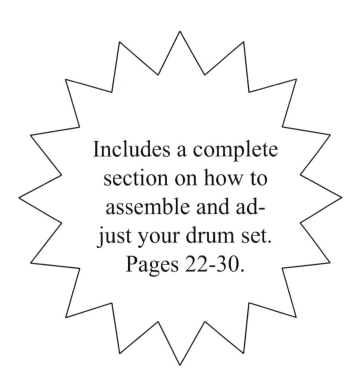

Includes a complete section on how to assemble and adjust your drum set. Pages 22-30.

ASSEMBLING THE DRUM SET

Before you begin to assemble your drum set, make sure all of the components are accounted for. The standard 5 piece kit consists of the following components:

Bass Drum   Snare Drum   Hi Tom   Medium Tom   Floor Tom

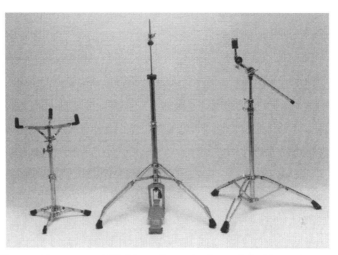

Snare Drum   Hi Hat Cymbal   Ride/Crash Cymbal
Stand   Stand   Stand

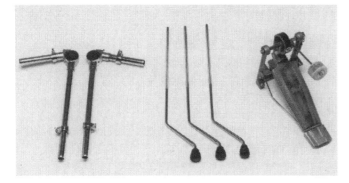

Tom Mounting   Floor Tom   Bass Drum   Hi Hat   Ride   Crash
Arms   Legs   Pedal   Cymbals   Cymbal   Cymbal

1. ASSEMBLE THE BASS DRUM

Note: We recommend that you set up your drum set on a carpeted area which will prevent it from sliding as you play.

A: Rotate the bass drum legs so that the rubber tips rest on the floor. Tighten the adjustment knobs to prevent the legs from moving. The front rim should sit about one inch above the floor. (Some models require the legs to be inserted into the bass drum).

B: Attach the bass drum pedal to the bass drum rim on the playing side (opposite the legs). Tighten the pedal's wingnut so that the pedal does not slide when flexed.

Wing Nut

Mounting Arms

C: Slide the tom mounting arms into the mounting brackets on top of the bass drum. Adjust the arms so that they look like handlebars which point toward the rear of the bass drum (playing side).

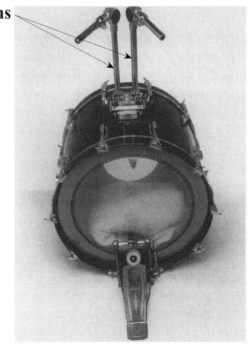

2. MOUNT THE HI TOM & MEDIUM TOM

Hi Tom

Medium Tom

A: Slide the hi tom onto the left mounting arm. Adjust the tom so that it will be angled toward you as you play.

B: Tighten the wingnut on the tom's mounting bracket so that the tom will not move.

C: Slide the medium tom onto the right mounting arm and follow the same steps as above.

3. ASSEMBLE THE FLOOR TOM

Wing Nut   Legs

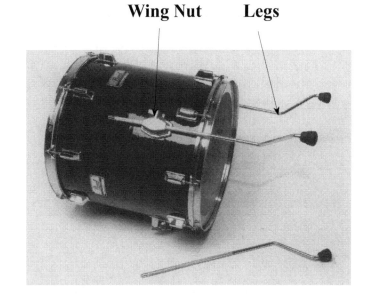

A: Loosen the wingnuts on the floor tom's leg mounting brackets so that the legs will slide in smoothly.

B: Slide the legs through the floor tom mounting brackets and tighten the wingnuts so the legs don't move or slide.

C: Place the floor tom to the 5 o'clock position of the bass drum.

Note: Many drummers prefer to angle the floor tom toward them which makes it easier to strike.

Floor Tom

4. SEAT THE SNARE DRUM

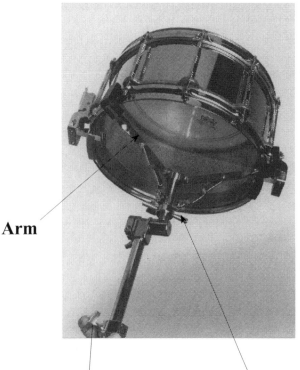

Arm

**Height Adjustment
Knob**

Arm Adjustment

A: Open the arms and legs of the snare drum stand. Tighten the height adjustment knob when the stand is at the desired height. The drum should sit at about waist level when you play.

B: Seat the snare drum on the stand with the snare wires facing the floor.

C: If your stand has an arm adjustment, turn it clockwise until the arms are snug against the snare drum rim.

D: Place the snare drum behind the drum set, approximately below the hi tom.

Snare Drum

5. ASSEMBLE THE HI HAT CYMBALS

Hi hats are two cymbals put together. Usually the cymbals are labelled "Top Hi Hat" and "Bottom Hi Hat".

A: Open and adjust the hi hat stand. The pedal should sit firmly on the floor.

B: Place the bottom hi hat on the stand. It should sit on a felt pad.

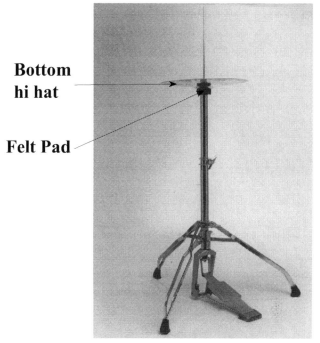

Bottom hi hat

Felt Pad

C: Attach the top hi hat cymbal to the hi hat clutch. A felt pad should be placed above and below the cymbal. The nut should be tightened so that it is snug against the felt pad.

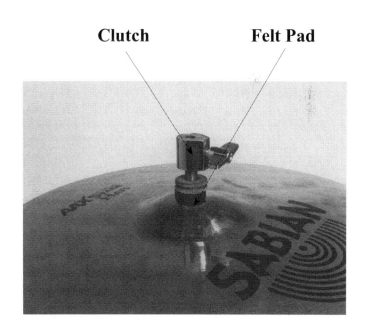

Clutch   **Felt Pad**

27

D: Slide the hi hat clutch onto the rod which protrudes from the top of the hi hat stand. Tighten the clutch's wingnut. (The cymbals should be spaced about an inch apart).

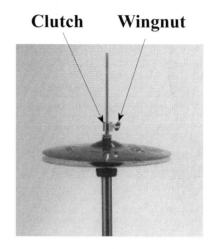

Clutch   Wingnut

Hi Hat

E: Place the hi hat to the left of the snare drum.

6. ASSEMBLE THE RIDE & CRASH CYMBALS

A: Loosen the adjustment knobs and extend the stand to the desired height.

B: Loosen the wing nut at the top of the stand and remove the top felt pad.

Adjustment Knobs

Bottom Felt Pad

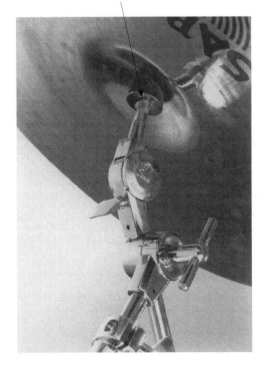

Wingnut   **Top Felt Pad**

C: Place the cymbal onto the stand. It should sit on the bottom felt pad.

D: Replace the top felt pad and attach the wing nut to the top of the stand. The nut should be snug against the top felt pad.

29

Crash   **Ride**

E: Place the ride cymbal to the right side of the Floor Tom. Place the crash cymbal toward the left front side of the Hi Tom.

7. ASSEMBLE THE DRUM THRONE

Note: For a discussion of tuning the drum set, refer to page 45 in the Appendix.

NOTATION

Let's take a look at how drum set music is written.

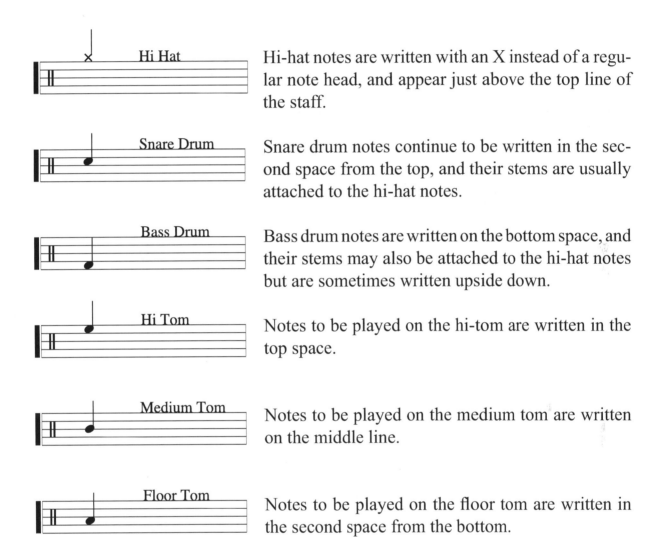

Hi-hat notes are written with an X instead of a regular note head, and appear just above the top line of the staff.

Snare drum notes continue to be written in the second space from the top, and their stems are usually attached to the hi-hat notes.

Bass drum notes are written on the bottom space, and their stems may also be attached to the hi-hat notes but are sometimes written upside down.

Notes to be played on the hi-tom are written in the top space.

Notes to be played on the medium tom are written on the middle line.

Notes to be played on the floor tom are written in the second space from the bottom.

BEAT #1

The first beat you will learn is used in many rock & roll songs. We will begin with the hi-hat, then add the snare and bass to build a beat.

1st: With your right stick, play several measures of eighth notes on the hi-hat cymbal. (Remember to count as you play). Keep the hi hat pedal down and the cymbals closed. Later you can experiment with opening and closing the hi hats as you play.

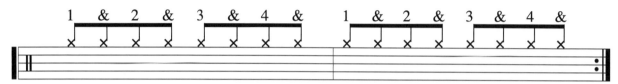

2nd: Now we will add the snare drum. You will strike the snare drum with the left stick on beats 2 and 4. (The hi-hat will be played with the snare).

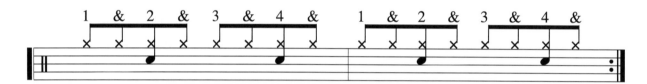

3rd: Next we will play the bass drum and the hi-hat. Using your right foot on the bass drum pedal, play the bass drum on beats 1 and 3. (The hi-hat will play with the bass drum).

4th: Now we will combine the hi-hat, snare, and bass drum to create a basic rock & roll beat. Remember, the bass plays on 1 & 3, while the snare plays on 2 & 4.

Note: You may have a good understanding of this beat, but have trouble playing it. Here are a few tips:

* Practice the beat slowly. If you try to go too fast, you will make mistakes and get frustrated. It is much easier to speed it up later.

* Make sure you are counting while you play.

* If you are having trouble with the bass drum part, it could be that you are not using good pedal technique. Keep your foot high on the pedal and don't allow the pedal to be out of control between beats.

You should take time to practice Beat #1. When you are ready, play along with Song #1 on the Video or Audio Tracks.

SONG 1

BEAT #2

In this beat, we will keep the same hi-hat and snare part we used in Beat #1. We will spice up the bass drum part by adding a note to the & of beat 3.

1st: Practice the hi-hat and bass drum parts together.

2nd: Now add the snare drum to beats 2 and 4.

You should take time to get comfortable with this beat. Then play along with Song #2 on the Video or Audio Tracks.

SONG 2

BEAT #3

In this beat, we will once again keep the same hi hat and snare parts. This time, we will add another bass drum note on the & of beat 1 (just like we did earlier on beat 3).

1st: Practice the hi-hat and bass drum parts together.

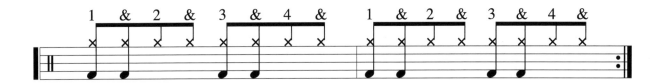

2nd: Add the snare drum to beats 2 and 4.

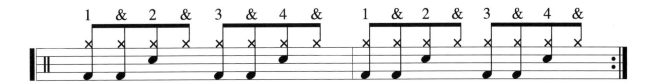

After you are comfortable with playing Beat #3 at a faster tempo, play along with Song #3 on the Video or Audio Tracks.

SONG 3

BEAT #4

This beat is a bit more challenging. The bass drum will be played on beat 1, the & of beat 2, and beat 3.

1st: Practice the hi hat and bass drum parts together.

2nd: Now add the snare drum to beats 2 and 4.

Take time to practice this beat. When you can play it at a faster tempo, play along with Song #4 on the Video or Audio Tracks.

SONG 4

TWO MEASURE BEATS

Many popular songs use two measure beats which are repeated throughout the song. We will create some two measure beats by combining Beats #1- 4 in various ways.

EXERCISE 29 - BEATS #1 AND #2

EXERCISE 30 - BEATS #1 AND #3

EXERCISE 31 - BEATS #2 AND #3

EXERCISE 32 - BEATS #2 AND #4

DRUM FILLS

Drum fills are used to add excitement to songs and to emphasize particular parts. Fills usually incorporate the toms and often use sixteenth notes.

FILL #1

The first fill you will learn is very popular. Four sixteenth notes will be played on each drum, starting with the snare drum, then hi tom, medium tom, and floor tom. The sticking will be R L R L, which ensures that you won't have to cross the left hand over the right hand as you move around the set.

You should practice this fill by creating a four bar phrase, which means that you will play a beat for three measures, then play the fill as the fourth measure. Immediately after the fill, you should begin the beat again and repeat the phrase several times. Any of the beats you have learned in this section will work as the first 3 measures. We are going to use Beat #2.

FILL #2

This time we will create a drum fill by using eighth and sixteenth notes. The progression around the set (snare, then hi tom, medium tom, and floor tom) will be the same. The rhythm will be counted 1 e & a 2 & 3 e & a 4 &. The sticking will be R L R L R L R L R L R L.

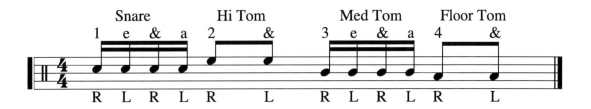

Now practice this fill by creating a four bar phrase. Play a beat for three measures, then play this fill as the fourth measure. Again, any of the beats you have learned will work as the first 3 measures. We are going to use Beat #2 again.

FILL #3

This fill will be similar to Fill #2, but this time we will switch the eighth and sixteenth notes. Now the rhythm will be counted 1 & 2 e & a 3 & 4 e & a. The sticking will be R L R L R L R L R L R L.

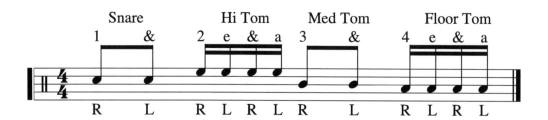

The fill should be practiced in the context of a 4 bar phrase. We will use Beat #2 again for the first three measures.

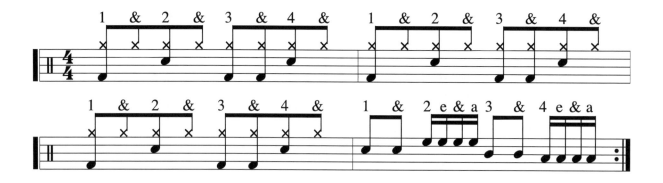

CREATING A 12 BAR PHRASE

Using a 4 bar phrase is an effective way to practice drum fills. When playing songs, however, a fill every 4 bars would be too repetitive and would not allow the song to flow properly. Using a 12 bar phrase can be more effective for playing songs. (Fills may also be effective at the end of a 16, 24, or 32 bar phrase). To create a 12 bar phrase, we will play a beat for 11 measures, then insert a drum fill as the 12th measure. Any of the beats and fills you have learned in Section IV will work. We are going to use Beat #2 and Fill #1.

After you are comfortable with the 12 bar sequence, you should listen to song #5 on the Video or Audio Tracks. Notice how the fill fits into the song, sort of like a period at the end of a sentence.

SONG 5

41

SUMMARY

This concludes the text of the *Drum Primer with Video & Audio Access*. Go back and review all of this material and practice it along with the Video until you understand it thoroughly. You should also study all of the material in the Appendix and make sure you understand it.

We have an excellent follow up course:

Drum Styles book by Tim Wimer is the follow up course to the *Drum Primer*. You'll quickly learn to play many different styles of music, such as Rock, Blues, Latin, Jazz, and Reggae, along with many exciting drum fills. Each section starts with the basic beats, adding one hand or foot at a time, then goes through several variations. It also covers drum fills in each style and applies this to songs where the student plays along with a full band on the online audio tracks. This is the perfect course for the intermediate to advanced drum student.

This book is available on Amazon.com. For any questions or problems, contact us at:

Watch & Learn, Inc.
2947 East Point St
East Point, GA 30344
800-416-7088
sales@cvls.com

QUICK REFERENCE CHART

A Quick Reference Chart has been included to make practicing and reviewing more convenient. This chart will also help you to track your progress as you master the material in this book.

RUDIMENTS

THE SINGLE STROKE ROLL

THE DOUBLE STROKE ROLL

THE SINGLE PARADIDDLE

THE DOUBLE PARADIDDLE

THE TRIPLE PARADIDDLE

NOTES

WHOLE NOTES

(4 beats each)

HALF NOTES

(2 beats each)

QUARTER NOTES

(1 beat each)

EIGHTH NOTES

(1/2 beat each)

SIXTEENTH NOTES

(1/4 beat each)

44

TUNING

The pitch of your drums can be changed by loosening or tightening the tension rods with a drum key. Turning the rods clockwise stretches the head, raising the drum's pitch. Turning the rods counter clockwise loosens the head, lowering the drum's pitch.

Adjusting the pitch of the drums is known as tuning. Unlike guitar strings, which must be tuned to a specific pitch, drums may be tuned to whatever pitch the drummer prefers. However, there are guidelines you need to follow while tuning.

The size of the drum must be considered. Smaller drums are designed to be tuned to a higher pitch than larger drums, therefore, the hi tom should have a higher pitch than the medium tom, and the medium tom should have a higher pitch than the floor tom. The bass drum, being the largest drum, should have the lowest pitch.

Note: To prevent the toms from over-ringing, you may wish to purchase muffling devices, such as Dead Ringers or Zero Rings. They are inexpensive and fairly easy to install. You can get them at your local music store.

You will want to muffle your bass drum so that it produces a deep thud-like sound. Remove the tension rods, rim and head, then place a pillow or blanket inside. Make sure the pillow or blanket rests against the heads, which will prevent ringing.

Pillow or blanket

45

GENERAL TUNING

When tuning the drum, you should start by tuning the top head. Begin with the tension rod closest to you. Using your drum key, rotate the tension rod one full turn (rotate clockwise if you want to raise the pitch, counter clockwise if you want to lower the pitch). Next, locate the tension rod opposite from the one you just turned and use the key to rotate it one full turn. Follow the diagram below until all the rods have been rotated one full turn. Start with #1 lug, then go in order (2, 3, 4, etc.)

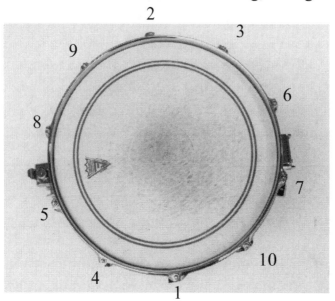

After all the rods have been rotated, go back to the first lug and repeat this process until the drum is at the desired pitch. As the drum head tightens, you will turn each lug less and less, from 1/2 turn to 1/16 of a turn. The idea is to apply the same amount of pressure evenly around the drum head, which helps to not only get the drum in tune, but also to prevent damage to the drum head.

FINE TUNING

When the drum is at the desired pitch, you are ready to fine tune, which ensures that the drum is in tune with itself. To do this, use a drum stick to tap the drum head about one inch to the inside of each tension rod. As you move around the drum head, listen for any changes in pitch. If you notice any pitch changes, rotate that tension rod slightly until it matches the pitch of the others. You may have to tap around the head several times before all the pitches are the same.

TUNING THE BOTTOM HEAD

Once the top head has been tuned, use the same procedure to tune the drum's bottom head. The bottom head should be tuned to the same pitch as the top head.

TUNING THE SNARE DRUM

While tuning your snare drum, you should flip the strainer to the down position so that the snare wires do not vibrate against the bottom head. The tom sound will help you to better hear the drum's pitch. After the heads have been tuned, flip the strainer to the up position again and use the strainer adjustment knob to set the desired tension of the snare wires. Turning the adjustment knob clockwise will increase the wire's tension against the bottom head, producing more of a snare sound. Turning the knob counter clockwise decreases the wire's tension against the bottom head, producing less of a snare sound. If you have questions about the sound of your snare drum, contact your local music store.

CONCLUSION

As you become more confident in your abilities, keep in mind the role of a band's drummer. The drummer's primary job is to keep a steady beat for the rest of the band. It is your job to keep other musicians from speeding up or slowing down.

As you develop drum parts for songs, keep the principle of simplicity in mind. In addition to being steady, your beats should also be clear and easy to follow. Too often, drummers overplay, squeezing too many fills into songs and muddying the music.

You should now work on expanding your repertoire by working through other books and DVDs, playing along with CD's, and playing with other musicians. Above all, develop the proper attitude as a drummer and enjoy being a part of the music.

Made in United States
Orlando, FL
15 April 2024

45836295R00030